Earth's Changing
Mountains

by Neil Morris

Raintree

www.raintreepublishers.co.uk
Visit our website to find out more information about **Raintree** books.

To order:
☎ Phone 44 (0) 1865 888112
🖹 Send a fax to 44 (0) 1865 314091
💻 Visit the Raintree Bookshop at **www.raintreepublishers.co.uk** to browse our catalogue and order online.

First published in Great Britain by Raintree,
Halley Court, Jordan Hill, Oxford OX2 8EJ,
part of Harcourt Education.
Raintree is a registered trademark of Harcourt
Education Ltd.

Editorial: Nick Hunter and Catherine Clarke
Design: Michelle Lisseter and Bridge Creative
Services Ltd
Picture Research: Maria Joannou and Liz Eddison
Illustrations: Bridge Creative Services Ltd
Production: Jonathan Smith

Originated by Dot Gradations Ltd
Printed and bound in China by South China
Printing Company

ISBN 1 844 21396 X
07 06 05
10 9 8 7 6 5 4 3 2

British Library Cataloguing in Publication Data
Morris, Neil
Earth's Changing Mountains. – (Landscapes and People)
551.4'32
A full catalogue record for this book is available
from the British Library.

Acknowledgements
The publishers would like to thank the following
for permission to reproduce photographs:
Alamy Images p. **17**; Corbis pp. **4** (Phil
Schermeister), **13** (Phil Schermeister), **15**, **24**, **27**
(Sygma/Jacques Langevin); Getty Images (Stone)
pp. **21**, **23**; Natural Science Photos pp. **9**
(Richard Revels), **12** (Pete Oxford), **18** (Pete
Oxford); NHPA pp. **10** (Daryl Balfour), **16** (Nigel
J. Dennis), **26** (A.N.T); Oxford Scientific Films
pp. **6** (Harold E. Wilson), **20** (Colin Monteath),
25 (David Simonson), **29** (Rick Price/SAL).

Cover photograph of mountains in Bern,
Switzerland, with permission of Eye Ubiquitous
(Jill Swainson).

The publishers would like to thank
Margaret Mackintosh for her assistance
in the preparation of this book.

Every effort has been made to contact copyright
holders of any material reproduced in this book.
Any omissions will be rectified in subsequent
printings if notice is given to the publishers.

Contents

Any words appearing in the text in bold, **like this**, are explained in the Glossary.

What are mountains?

What do you think of when you think of a mountain? Is it steep and rocky, with daring climbers clinging to its sides as they slowly make their way to the top? Or is it full of grassy slopes, where sheep **graze** and colourful mountain flowers grow? Whichever one you think of, you're right. A mountain can be both of these things, and many others too.

All mountains are parts of Earth's surface that stand high above their surroundings. Smaller rises are usually called hills. Some mountains are very steep and form high, pointed **peaks**. Others have a more rounded shape, though the top of these mountains may be just as high.

A mountain may be a single peak, but mountains are often joined together in a mountain **range**. Some ranges have hundreds of separate peaks. When ranges are grouped together, they are sometimes called a mountain **chain**.

At 1917 metres, Mount Washington is the highest peak in New Hampshire, USA. This mountain is in the Presidential Range, which forms part of the larger White Mountains chain. They both belong to a mountain system called the Appalachians.

World of mountains

There are mountains all over the world, with major ranges on every **continent**. There is even a high mountain range in Antarctica, the icy continent that lies around the South Pole. It stretches 3500 kilometres (nearly 2200 miles) across the frozen land.

This world map shows the location of the ten longest mountain ranges. The longest of all, the Andes, stretches for 7200 kilometres (4470 miles) down the whole of South America. Its peaks form parts of seven different countries.

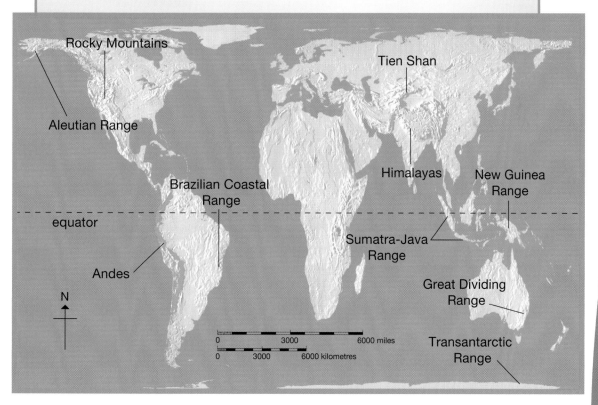

Looking at mountains

Mountains are formed in different ways and are shaped by wind and weather. There are many different kinds of mountains, including explosive **volcanoes**, which can cause major changes in the surrounding **landscape**.

People live on, use and change mountains as well. In recent years **industry** and **tourism** have had a great effect on many of the world's mountain ranges. In some places this has brought problems.

How are mountains formed?

Mountains are formed over long periods of time by the movement of rocks beneath Earth's surface. This surface is part of our planet's rocky outer layer, which is called Earth's **crust**. The crust is not one continuous layer, like the shell of an egg, but is broken into several huge pieces. We call these pieces **tectonic plates**.

Jigsaw of plates

Earth's plates fit together like a giant jigsaw, with the two sides of each plate close up against each other. The plates are not still – they are always moving, very slowly, by just a few centimetres each year. This means that some edges of the plates push against each other, and as they do, they buckle (bend) at the edges. Over many thousands of years, this pressing and bending push mountains up from Earth's surface.

This active, smoking volcano lies on one of the Aleutian islands of Alaska, USA. The islands are part of the Ring of Fire (see page 7).

Volcanoes

Beneath Earth's crust there is a thick layer called the mantle. The rocks here are so hot that some of them have melted, making them runny like sticky toffee. In some places where one plate is forced beneath another, the hot, **molten** rock forces its way through a crack in Earth's crust and forms an erupting **volcano**. Once it is on the surface, the molten rock cools and hardens again. If this goes on happening at the same spot for many thousands of years, the rocks build up to form a volcanic cone or a mountain. When a volcano has not erupted for many years, it is said to be dormant, or 'sleeping'. After thousands of years, it may be called extinct, or 'dead' – but the mountains formed by these volcanoes still remain.

Shifting ground

There are a lot of volcanoes around the edge of the Pacific Ocean. This circle of tectonic plate boundaries around the Pacific is called the **Ring of Fire** (see the map below). Throughout this whole area, erupting volcanoes change the **landscape**. In 1980, for example, a volcano in the Cascade Range in Washington state, USA, erupted. A huge explosion blew 400 metres off the top of Mount St Helens. The surrounding area was covered in volcanic ash and rock. Before that day, Mount St Helens had been dormant for 123 years.

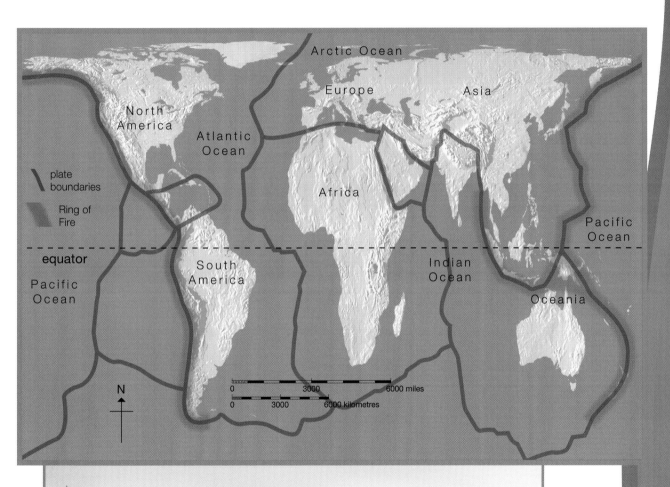

*This map shows the world's major plates. As the plates move – very, very slowly – they change the shape of **continents** and create mountains. There are mountain ranges on the ocean floor, too. A huge range, called the Mid-Atlantic Ridge, stretches right down the middle of the Atlantic Ocean. Here, the plates are moving apart, allowing molten rock to force its way through and form mountains.*

7

Folds and faults

Earth's plates are made up of layers of rock. As the plates move, the layers of rock are squeezed and crumpled into folds. The world's biggest mountain **ranges** were all made this way over millions of years. Some of them, such as the Himalayas, are still being folded and pushed up. This means they get a tiny bit higher every year.

Sometimes the rock layers are pushed and folded so much that they cannot bend any more. Then they break and form a crack called a **fault**. Different kinds of mountains, including **volcanoes**, form along a fault.

fold mountain

block mountain

fault

As mountains fold up (left), they leave valleys between them. Fold mountains have pointed or rounded peaks. Block mountains appear between faults in the surface of Earth, and they usually have a flat top.

Different shapes

Fold mountains are caused by squeezing and crumpling. The top parts of the folds become mountains, and the lower parts between them are **valleys**. The Appalachians, in the eastern USA (see page 13), are fold mountains. So too are the European Alps, which are much younger. They formed about 50 million years ago.

When a piece of Earth's crust fractures (cracks), layers of rock are sometimes pushed up between two faults. These are called block (or fault-block) mountains. Examples are the Teton Range, in Wyoming, USA, which formed about 10 million years ago; and the Harz Mountains, in Germany, which are much older.

Dome mountains are formed when the top layers of Earth's crust are pushed up by **molten** rock underneath. This creates a big bulge (or dome) on the surface. The Black Hills, in South Dakota, USA, are dome mountains. They were pushed up about 65 million years ago.

*Layers of rock are called **strata**. It is easy to see here, on the south coast of England, how the strata have been squeezed and folded. Rocks are very hard materials, so imagine the force that was needed to change these strata.*

Changing landscapes

Air cools as it rises, so the higher the mountain, the colder the temperature at its **peak**. This is why high mountains are covered in snow, even in the hottest parts of the world. In the East African country of Tanzania, for example, the climate is hot and tropical. Yet the country's highest mountain, Kilimanjaro, is so high (5895 metres) that it is cold enough for snow to stay at the top all year round.

Mount Kilimanjaro, in East Africa, is a dormant volcano. Although it is very cold at the top of the mountain, the lower slopes make good farming land. Kilimanjaro is surrounded by wildlife parks, in Tanzania and Kenya.

Rain shadow

High mountain **ranges** affect rainfall in surrounding regions. This is because winds in mountainous regions usually blow from one direction, bringing clouds with them. As the clouds rise to pass over the mountains, they cool down and drop rain or snow on the slopes below. This means that the windward side of a mountain – the slope that has the wind blowing towards it – is often wet. When the winds reach the other side, they have lost their moisture and are dry. Because of this, the leeward, or sheltered, side of a mountain – where the wind is blowing away – receives much less rain. We call this a rain shadow.

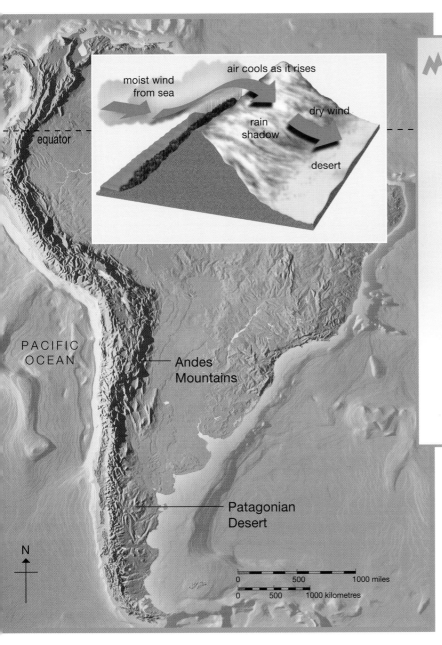

air cools as it rises

moist wind
from sea

rain
shadow

dry wind

desert

equator

PACIFIC
OCEAN

Andes
Mountains

Patagonian
Desert

N

0   500   1000 miles

0   500   1000 kilometres

As moist winds from the Pacific Ocean pass over the western side of the Andes Mountains, in South America, it often rains. On the eastern side of the mountains, the air no longer holds enough water to rain. In this region of southern Argentina, the rain shadow has helped to create the dry Patagonian Desert.

Mountain winds

As wind flows down mountain slopes, it warms up quickly. In the European Alps, a dry wind blows down the northern slopes. As the wind warms up, it can cause snow to melt and slide down the mountainside in dangerous **avalanches**. On the eastern side of the Rocky Mountains, in North America, similar mountain winds are known as chinooks (and sometimes as snow eaters). A chinook that drops 1000 metres down a mountain may warm up by as much as 10°Celsius. This makes it easy to understand why areas that have dry or chinook winds are generally warm.

Weathering

Mountains change over long periods of time. Some mountain **ranges** are still being pushed higher by **tectonic plate** movements, while others are very slowly getting smaller. Their **peaks** are lower than they once were, because the effects of weather have worn them away. Wind, rain and ice gradually break down rocks, in a process called **weathering**. Eventually, small pieces of rock are carried away down the mountain.

Rain and snow

Water causes many changes to mountain **landscapes**. It is cold near the top of a high mountain. This means that there is often a lot of snow rather than rainfall, and any running water quickly freezes. It often freezes in cracks in rocks. It expands when it freezes and this splits the rock and helps to break it into little pieces. Lower down the mountain, where it is usually warmer, water runs in tiny streams, which flow together to make rivers. The force of this moving water washes away pieces of rock, carrying them down the mountain.

This glacier is moving down from high mountain peaks in south-west Argentina.

Rivers of ice

Near the top of some mountains, snow piles up in the cold air and turns to ice. Eventually, the thick layer of ice begins to slide slowly down the side of the mountain. It forms a river of ice, called a **glacier**. Many glaciers travel less than 1 metre a day, but as they move, they drag pieces of rock with them. The rocks, **boulders** and stones grind against the mountain beneath the glacier. Over thousands of years, the glacier cuts a deeper and deeper U-shaped **valley** in the mountain.

Old mountains

The Appalachian Mountains stretch for about 2400 kilometres (1490 miles) down the eastern side of the USA. They were squeezed up around 300 million years ago and are the oldest mountains in North America. Scientists believe that the Appalachians were formed when tectonic plates moved towards each other and caused rock layers to fold up (see page 8). When they first formed, the mountains must have had high, jagged peaks. In the millions of years since then, however, the peaks have been **eroded**, making them more smooth and rounded. The range's highest point is 2037 metres above **sea level**, at the top of Mount Mitchell, in North Carolina.

Changing life

Imagine you are a mountaineer, climbing to the highest **peaks** of a mountain. On your way to the top, you would see that growing conditions for plants change. These conditions change with the seasons, too. On mountains, just as lower down, most plant growth takes place in spring and summer. Then the days are long and warm. In winter, it is generally too cold for plants to grow, especially on the higher slopes.

The forest zone

The lowest slopes of the mountain (known as the forest zone) may be warm enough for **broad-leaved trees**, such as oak and ash, to grow. These kinds of trees need warm summers and mild winters, so they cannot grow higher up the mountain, where the weather is colder. Instead, the upper part of the forest zone is often covered with **conifers**, such as pine and fir. These evergreen trees have strong, needle-shaped leaves, and their roots spread out well in the thin soil. They can survive long winters, when the slopes are frozen hard. Where trees have been cut down, there may be grassy **alpine meadows**. Mountain farmers use these meadows for grazing their animals.

The forest zone is below the tree line. Only small plants grow above the tree line. Bare rock leads up to the snow line. Higher than this, there is always snow.

tree line

snow line

Above the tree line

The upper limit of the forest zone is called the **tree line** (or timber line). Above this level, it is too cold and windy for trees to live. Most soil here is quickly blown away. Only tough grasses and low flowering alpine plants grow above the tree line. Higher still, you will find just mosses and lichens growing.

Above the snow line

High mountains have snow on their peaks all year round. Above a certain level, called the **snow line**, there is always a layer of snow on the slopes. In warm regions of the world, the snow line is very high up. Mount Kilimanjaro in tropical Africa (see page 10) is a good example of this. In colder regions, near the North and South Poles, the snow line is lower down the mountain.

These tough conditions have affected animals, as well as trees and plants, because there is very little food for them on mountains. For the same reason, people rarely live above the lower slopes.

These cows are grazing on an alpine meadow in Switzerland. There is snow on the peaks, and the animals move down the mountain in winter (see page 21).

15

Adapting to the mountains

Some animals have **adapted** to life in the difficult conditions of the mountains. Many, such as mountain goats, have a thick coat to keep them warm during the severe winter. Mountain goats are able to climb along rocky **crags**, but they move down to the lower slopes in winter. Other animals, such as alpine marmots, don't move down the slopes but dig burrows and sleep through the winter. Mountain hares and some birds change the colour of their coat or feathers during winter, from brown to white so that they are not easily seen by **predators** against the snowy background.

The lammergeier, or bearded vulture, lives in the Pyrenees Mountains of Europe as well as the Himalayas. It is famous for breaking open the bones of dead animals, which it finds on the slopes. The lammergeier carries a bone up to a great height and drops it on to rocks below, splitting it open to get at the juicy marrow inside.

Mountain cats

Two of the world's big cats have adapted to life in the mountains. Mountain lions (also called pumas or cougars) are found in North and South America, but they have become rare wherever people have taken over the **landscape**. In the USA, the pumas that survive live in the mountains of the west. They are quite happy at high **altitude**, and have been found on mountains 4500 metres high.

The snow leopard, as its name suggests, lives in the cold mountains of central Asia. It is at home on rocky slopes, ice and snow. It has long, thick fur to keep it warm. High up in the cold mountains, the snow leopard hunts a type of wild sheep known as blue sheep, wild goats and small musk deer. In heavy snow and very cold weather, a snow leopard will move down into the **valleys** to find food.

Llamas are used to carry loads in the Andes of South America.

Ox of Tibet

The yak is a wild ox of Asia. It lives high up in the mountains of Tibet, where winter temperatures drop well below freezing. It is a big animal – up to 1.8 metres high at the shoulders – with long horns. It is used to living on the mountains, and despite its size, is light-footed and can even slide down icy slopes. Many years ago the farmers of the region (see page 20) realized that the yak could be useful to them in many ways. They use yaks to carry heavy loads, as well as keeping them for their milk.

Changing settlements

You might think that people would not want to live high up in the mountains. It is certainly true that the world's mountainous regions are generally much less **populated** than the lowlands. These regions are difficult to get to, and it's hard work walking uphill all the time! Nevertheless, some of our early human **ancestors** settled in the mountains. Perhaps they followed rivers upstream and uphill, so that they always had a constant supply of water. Later, people found that **settlements** built on high ground were easier to protect. Mountain settlers could see others coming and take action if they wanted to keep them away.

High up in the Andes Mountains, this Aymara woman rows her reed boat on Lake Titicaca. The shores of the lake were once part of the Inca Empire.

Ancient Andean cultures

People first settled in the Andes Mountains of South America many thousands of years ago. Their ancestors had travelled to North America from Asia and moved south. By about 5000 BC people were keeping some of the mountain animals that previously they had hunted, such as alpacas and llamas. They kept herds of animals near their settlements, which meant there was always a supply of milk and meat, as well as skins for clothing. Some people then began farming, growing maize and potatoes. By about 1000 BC there was widespread settlement in the Andes.

Around Lake Titicaca

Lake Titicaca lies at a height of 3811 metres above **sea level** in the Andes on the border between Peru and Bolivia. It is one of the highest lakes in the world. Its shores and islands are home to the Aymara people, who traditionally live by farming and fishing in the lake from boats made of reeds. The Aymara have lived here for many centuries, and some manage to carry on their traditional way of life today.

The Incas

The greatest of the ancient **Andean** cultures was the Inca **civilization**. They founded a capital at Cuzco around AD 1100, and then developed from a small tribe into an organized people under one ruler, called the Inca. They began to conquer neighbouring lands, until they had a population of millions. Mountain **peaks** were sacred to the Incas, and they sometimes made human sacrifices in the high Andes.

0   500   1000 miles

0   500   1000 kilometres

equator

Andes

Cuzco •

Lake Titicaca

N

Inca Empire

Mountain farmers

Farming in the mountains is hard work. The biggest problem is finding flat land, for growing crops and grazing animals. The Incas (see page 19) overcame this problem by turning the slopes of the Andes into **terraces** of flat fields for farming. In order to do this, they even had to carry soil up from the **valleys** below. They laid the soil flat and built walls to protect their fields and stop them from slipping down the mountain slopes.

In the high Himalayas of Nepal, Sherpa villagers and farmers find yaks are useful not only for their milk, which can be turned into butter, but also for their meat.

In the Himalayas

The mountain-dwelling Sherpa people of Nepal are used to life in the high Himalayas. Some of their villages are over 3500 metres above **sea level**, and they have summer **settlements** even higher up, where they live when the weather is warmer. The Sherpas raise yaks, and their farming villages are surrounded by terraced fields of barley, buckwheat, potatoes and radishes. During the 20th century many Sherpas used their knowledge of the Himalayan **peaks** to become mountaineering guides. In 1953 a Sherpa, Tenzing Norgay, was one of the first two men to climb to the top of Everest, the world's highest mountain.

Up and down the mountain

In the alpine regions of Switzerland, Austria and other European countries, mountain farmers live by the seasons. In summer, when the grass is fresh and green, dairy farmers **graze** their cattle on the high **alpine meadows** above the farming villages. In autumn, before the first snows fall and cover the meadows, the farmers bring their animals back down the mountain. The cattle spend winter inside sheds on the farm, to protect them from the cold. The growth of **tourism** in the region means that this alpine farming is slowing dying out.

Rice terraces

The Ifugao people of northern Luzon, the largest island in the Philippines, are rice-growers. They are famous for their terraced fields, surrounded by high stone walls, which cling to the slopes of their mountainous region. Some of the walls were built long ago by their **ancestors**, who learned how to bring water to the terraces through a clever system of pipes. They live in small villages of five to ten houses scattered among the fields.

Sun and snow

Weather changes are usually greater in the mountains than at lower levels. In many mountainous regions, it is hot and sunny in the summer, but very cold in winter. This has a great effect on **tourism**. In summer, many people like to take their holidays in mountain towns and villages, where they can walk or hike and enjoy the beautiful scenery. In winter, the hotels, guesthouses and apartments in the same towns will be full of people who enjoy skiing and other winter sports. Many mountain resorts have **adapted** very successfully to this seasonal approach.

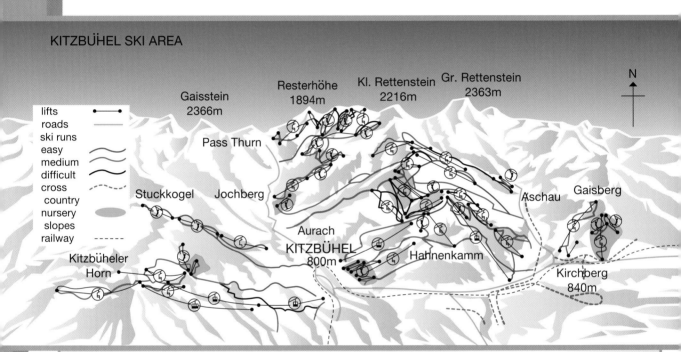

KITZBÜHEL SKI AREA

The town of Kitzbühel has a permanent population of just 8200 people. Above the town there are 164 kilometres (102 miles) of ski runs, served by 59 ski lifts. On the map the black ski runs are difficult, the red are medium and the blue runs are supposed to be easy (if you are a good skier!).

A changing mountain town

The town of Kitzbühel, in the Austrian Alps, was founded in the 12th century. It once belonged to Bavarian dukes and bishops, who built a church there in 1373. In the 16th century nearby silver and copper mines made the townspeople rich. The last mine closed in 1770. The town probably changed little between then and the middle of the 20th century, when Kitzbühel became famous as a growing ski resort. Today, it is one of the most popular resorts, and many of the old buildings have been converted into hotels. Every year the town stages the Hahnenkamm downhill race, which is one of the most famous ski-races in the world.

Mile High City

Because it stands at 1609 metres above **sea level**, the US city of Denver, capital of Colorado, is known as the 'Mile High City'. It was founded in the **foothills** of the Rocky Mountains during the **gold rush** of 1859, when people went there in search of gold and a fortune. Few **prospectors** made much money, but gold and silver were found in the mountains. Business grew and a railway reached the town in 1870. Cattle and sheep **ranchers** settled beside the town, which by 1900 had more than 100,000 citizens. Since then, Denver has grown dramatically. Tourists come to visit the Rocky Mountain National Park, with its lakes, fishing streams and trails. Nearby ski resorts, such as Vail and Aspen, made the city even more popular. In 1995 Denver international airport opened, helping business and tourism. The city now has a **population** of around half a million people.

The city of Denver is just south-east of Rocky Mountain National Park. It is less than 150 kilometres (95 miles) away from the highest peak in the Rockies, Mount Elbert (4399 metres).

Changing mountains

Some of the world's most valuable resources come from mountains. For this reason, many mountain regions have become centres of **industry**.

Using fast-flowing rivers

The fast-flowing rivers of mountainous regions are useful for producing electricity. In the Snowy Mountains, in south-east Australia, **dams** have been built on rivers so that water can be stored in **reservoirs**. Some of the water then flows down specially built tunnels and pipes. The water falls fast for hundreds of metres, driving **generators** to make electricity for Canberra, Australia's capital city. This industry changes the **landscape**. When dams are built, they flood **valleys**, destroying plants and other wildlife.

*The roots of trees help to hold soil in place, protecting it from the effects of weather. So, when trees are cut down – there is a much greater chance of soil **erosion**.*

Logging

Logging is the most important industry in many mountain areas. Thick forests of fir and other trees on the slopes of the Cascade **Range**, in north-west USA, are used to supply the timber industry. The mountain forests of the south-east Asian islands of Borneo and Sumatra are also being cut down for timber. This has meant that many rare animals of the mountain forests are threatened with losing their homes and perhaps dying out.

Mining the mountains

Metals and minerals are common in mountain areas. There are huge mines in many of the world's major mountain ranges. The world's largest **opencast** copper mine is in Chuquicamata, Chile (shown below). This mining town is on a **plateau** nearly 3000 metres up in the Andes Mountains. Further north in the Andes, there are many tin mines in Bolivia, where the mountains are also important for mining lead, silver and zinc. These mines create vast holes in the ground. They bring wealth to a region, but they also have a great effect on the landscape. It is not always possible to fill in the mines when they are no longer useful.

Another change caused by logging, and all forms of industry, is road building. Workers need roads in order to take equipment up the mountain and bring produce down. Building roads means that more trees are cut down, other plants are destroyed and soil is worn away. In many cases this leaves the slopes beside the roads bare and can lead to **landslides** and floods.

Cable cars and lifts

Skiing and other winter sports change mountain regions. One of the most obvious changes is the sight of cable cars and different forms of lifts, which take skiers and snowboarders up the mountains. In Kitzbühel (see page 22), for example, there are five cable cars. In 2002 the Winter Olympics were held on the mountain slopes near Salt Lake City, in Utah, USA. Many new runs and tracks were built for various winter sports.

Skiers enjoy the Snowy Mountains of north-east Victoria, Australia. These are the highest mountains in the Australian Alps.

Climbing and hiking

Mountaineering and rock climbing are popular sports. People enjoy the challenge of getting to the top of a mountain, often by the most difficult route. Today, there are many adventure holidays to remote mountain areas, such as the Andes and the Himalayas. Many people enjoy spending leisure time and holidays in the mountains, simply walking or hiking. All these activities have a great impact on mountains, as huts and even hotels are built for these adventurous mountaineers. Most do their best to leave the mountains as they found them, but changes to the natural environment are bound to occur.

Overusing the mountains

If too many people visit a mountain region, they can cause great damage. They might damage plants, and too many trampling feet can leave soil bare. The bare soil is then easily washed away by heavy rain. Skiing can have a similar effect, and skiing off-piste (that is, away from recognized, marked runs) can even disturb the snow and cause dangerous **avalanches**. Some other problems caused by tourists can easily be avoided. People should never leave litter, and they should be very careful with matches to make sure that they do not start forest fires.

Looking to the future

We all want to enjoy the mountains, but if we change them too much, there will be little left to enjoy. The governments of many countries tackle this problem by setting aside nature reserves and national parks, allowing local wildlife to thrive. These measures help mountain regions to go on developing and changing slowly and naturally. The forces of our planet mean that thousands of years from now, the world's mountains will look very different from the way they look today.

These rescue workers are searching for survivors after an avalanche at Galtür, in the Austrian Alps.

Mountain facts and figures

The world's longest mountain ranges

range	continent	length in km	length in miles
Andes	South America	7200	4474
Rockies	North America	4800	2983
Himalayas	Asia	3800	2361
Great Dividing Range	Australasia	3600	2237
Transantarctic Mountains	Antarctica	3500	2175
Brazilian Coastal Range	South America	3000	1864
Sumatra-Java Range	Asia	2900	1802
Aleutian Range	North America	2600	1616
Tien Shan	Asia	2200	1367
New Guinea Range	Asia	2000	1243

The world's highest mountains (all in the Himalayas, Asia)

mountain	height in m
Everest	8863
K2	8610
Kangchenjunga	8598
Lhotse	8511
Makalu I	8481
Dhaulagiri I	8167
Manaslu I	8156
Cho Oyu	8153
Nanga Parbat	8124
Annapurna I	8091

Highest mountains in each continent

mountain	continent	range	height in m
Everest	Asia	Himalayas	8863
Aconcagua	South America	Andes	6960
McKinley (Denali)	North America	Alaska Range	6194
Kilimanjaro	Africa	—	5895
Elbrus	Europe	Caucasus	5642
Vinson	Antarctica	Ellsworth	5140
Mount Wilhelm	Oceania	New Guinea Range	4509

N La Paz, the capital of Bolivia, was built on the site of an ancient Inca village. It lies high in the Andes Mountains, at 3632 metres, and is the world's highest capital city.

Worst avalanches of the 20th century

location	year	estimated deaths
Alps, Italy	1916	10,000
Huaraz, Peru	1941	5,000
Huascaran, Peru	1962	3,500
Chungar, Peru	1971	600
Blons, Austria	1954	411

Worst volcanic eruptions

location	year	estimated deaths
Tambora, Indonesia	1815	92,000
Miyi-Yama, Indonesia	1793	53,000
Mont Pelée, Martinique	1902	38,000
Krakatoa, Indonesia	1883	36,000
Nevado del Ruiz, Colombia	1985	23,000
Etna, Italy	1669	20,000
Vesuvius, Italy	79	20,000
Kelud, Indonesia	1586	10,000
Lamington, Papua New Guinea	1951	5,000

Glossary

adapt to change in order to suit the conditions

alpine meadow grassland on a high mountain, such as in the Alps of Europe

altitude height of a mountain (measured above sea level)

ancestor person who lived long ago, from whom someone is descended

Andean relating to the region of the Andes, a mountain range in South America

avalanche large fall of snow or rocks down a mountainside

boulder large stone that has been worn smooth

broad-leaved tree tree with wide, flat leaves instead of needles

chain group of mountain ranges

civilization advanced culture, or a people with an advanced culture

conifer tree with needle-like leaves that bears its seeds in cones

continent one of the world's seven huge land masses

crag steep, rugged rock

crust hard, outer layer of Earth

dam large barrier across a river that holds back water

earthquake sudden shaking of the ground caused by movements beneath Earth's surface

erode slowly wear away. Soil and rocks are eroded by the effects of the weather.

fault crack in Earth's crust

foothills lower hills around the edge of a mountain range

generator machine that turns one form of energy, such as the power of water, into electricity

glacier slowly moving mass of ice

gold rush large numbers of people moving to a region where gold has been found

graze to eat growing grass, or to feed animals on grass

industry business, often factories that make things

landscape natural scenery

landslide large fall of soil or rocks down a mountainside

logging cutting down trees for timber

molten melted (turned into liquid by heat)

opencast mine that is worked on, or just below, the surface – rather than deep underground

peak pointed top of a mountain

plateau flat area of high land

population total number of people who live in a particular place

predator animal that hunts and kills other animals for food

prospector person who explores a region for gold or other precious metal

rancher person who farms a cattle ranch

range series of mountains that form a group

reservoir man-made lake where water is collected and stored

Ring of Fire zone around the Pacific Ocean, where there are many active volcanoes at the edge of plates

sea level level of the sea's surface, which is used as zero in calculating the height of a mountain

settlement place where people live permanently

snow line height on a mountain above which there is always snow

strata layers of rock

tectonic plate huge piece of Earth's crust

terrace flat area of land cut into a slope to be used for growing things

tourism business of organizing holidays and visits to places of interest

tree line height on a mountain above which no tress grow

valley low area between mountains

volcano opening where molten rock and gas come from deep inside Earth, often forming a mountain

weathering wearing away of rocks by wind, rain and ice

Further reading

Biomes Atlases: Mountains, Tim Harris (Raintree, 2003)

Curriculum Visions: The Mountain Book, Brian Knapp (Atlantic Europe Publishing Co Ltd, 2000)

Earth Files: Mountains, Chris Oxlade (Heinemann Library, 2002)

Geography Detective: Mountains, Philip Sauvain (Zoe Books, 1996)

Geography for Fun: Mountains and Our Moving Earth, Pam Robson (Franklin Watts, 2001)

Mapping Earthforms: Mountains, Catherine Chambers (Heinemann Library, 2000)

Index

Titles in the Landscapes and People series include:

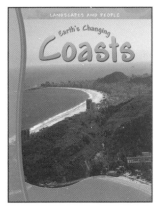

Hardback   1 844 21392 7

Hardback   1 844 21393 5

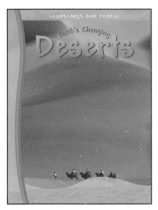

Hardback   1 844 21394 3

Hardback   1 844 21395 1

Hardback   1 844 21396 X

Hardback   1 844 21397 8

Find out about the other titles in this series on our website www.raintreepublishers.co.uk